After the Tests

U.S. Policy
Toward India and Pakistan

Report of an Independent Task Force

*Cosponsored by the Brookings Institution
and the Council on Foreign Relations*

Richard N. Haass and Morton H. Halperin,
Co-Chairs

CONTENTS

FOREWORD

In May 1998, both India and Pakistan conducted a series of nuclear weapons tests, and then each declared itself a nuclear power. In the aftermath of those tests, important questions for U.S. foreign policy remain; most importantly, what actions the United States should take to preserve stability in South Asia while stemming further nuclear proliferation elsewhere.

In this context, the Council on Foreign Relations and the Brookings Institution, while not taking positions as institutions on the issue, sponsored an independent Task Force to consider the consequences of the nuclear tests and to recommend the next steps for U.S. policy, hoping the group's conclusions might help stimulate debate in the United States, South Asia, and elsewhere. The Task Force was chaired by Richard N. Haass and Morton H. Halperin, both former senior government officials; its distinguished members included nuclear and South Asian experts with a wide variety of views and backgrounds.

Meeting twice over the summer of 1998, the Task Force used as a departure point for discussion the conclusions of another independent Task Force sponsored by the Council on Foreign Relations in 1996. In assessing U.S. policy toward India and Pakistan, that earlier group had concluded that it was an appropriate time for the United States to propose a closer strategic relationship with India—which it determined was poised to emerge as a major power—and to restore close relations with Pakistan. To that end, it recommended a series of specific policies that the U.S. government should adopt, such as holding regular, high-level meetings with Indian officials and extending credits for trade and investment in Pakistan.

Although the administration did take some steps in improving relations with these two countries, the Indian and then the Pakistani nuclear tests necessarily put this process on hold and in fact triggered the introduction of comprehensive sanctions. In this context, the 1998 Task Force turned its attention to the question of how the U.S. government could find a way to put its bilateral relations with India and Pakistan back on track while, at the same time, safeguarding its interests in the realm of nuclear nonproliferation.

Not surprisingly, some members disagreed over the degree to which the U.S. government should induce the Indian and Pakistani governments to adopt greater restrictions on their respective nuclear programs. However, despite their diversity, the members of the Task Force did concur that U.S. policy should encourage the governments of India and Pakistan to place visible, formal, and legally binding caps on their nuclear programs and to take steps to improve their bilateral relations. In that context, the group also urged Congress to provide the president with the flexibility to remove most sanctions, while keeping in place those barring the provision of technology that could potentially contribute to the Indian and Pakistani nuclear programs.

At the core of the Task Force's conclusions is the recognition that the United States has important interests in improving relations with India and Pakistan, in promoting regional stability, and in preventing further nuclear proliferation in South Asia and elsewhere. Given the tempestuous history of Indo-Pakistani relations, it would be dangerous to underestimate the impact that the tests could have on the region. Therefore, it is our hope that this report will contribute to a fuller understanding of the options for a successful U.S. policy in this uncertain period.

The Council on Foreign Relations would like to thank the W. Alton Jones Foundation, whose financial support helped make this project possible.

Michael H. Armacost
President, the Brookings Institution

Leslie H. Gelb
President, Council on Foreign Relations

After the Tests

U.S. Policy
Toward India and Pakistan

FINDINGS AND RECOMMENDATIONS

Less than two years ago, an independent Task Force similar to this one completed its assessment of American foreign policy toward India and Pakistan. "The end of the Cold War should permit a substantial improvement of bilateral relations between Washington and both New Delhi and Islamabad, as well as between the two principal South Asian states," the Task Force concluded in its report. "The time is ripe, in particular, for the United States to propose a closer strategic relationship with India, which has the potential to emerge as a full-fledged major power."[1]

In order to promote these ends, the previous Task Force made a number of specific recommendations. Toward India, the U.S. government was encouraged to hold regular high-level meetings; loosen unilateral constraints on dual-use technology exports; increase military cooperation; undertake limited arms sales; cooperate in the realm of energy, including civil nuclear power; and support India's membership in the Asia-Pacific Economic Forum. At the same time, the Task Force endorsed restoring normal and close relations with Pakistan, and favored extending credits to Pakistan for trade and investment; reducing its debt; providing economic and military aid; and allowing limited arms sales.

Some of these recommendations became reality as the policy of the Clinton administration (although not Congress) moved in the direction endorsed by the Task Force. That same Task Force recognized, however, that regional developments would inevitably and significantly influence the course of U.S. foreign policy. "The desire and ability of the United States to expand relations will clearly be affected by Indian and Pakistani behavior. . . . Destabilizing moves by either country would almost certainly restrict the pos-

---

[1] *A New U.S. Policy Toward India and Pakistan: Report of an Independent Task Force Sponsored by the Council on Foreign Relations* (New York: Council on Foreign Relations, 1997), p. 1, 3.

sibilities for cooperation and might even result in the reintroduction of selective, preferably multinational sanctions."[2]

This is just what has happened in the aftermath of decisions by India and then Pakistan to test nuclear devices in May 1998. The tests pose a difficult challenge for American foreign policy, which must now seek with considerable urgency to promote stability in the region, improve relations with both India and Pakistan, and minimize any adverse impact the nuclear tests may have on global nonproliferation objectives. Devising and implementing policies to advance these three objectives simultaneously promises to be no easy task. For this reason, the Council on Foreign Relations and the Brookings Institution decided to cosponsor a new independent Task Force of former government officials and individuals with expertise in both the region and nuclear matters to assess the implications of the tests and to recommend a course of action for the United States and other parties.

THE MAY 1998 TESTS

India's precise motives and reasons for testing nuclear devices on May 11 and 13 remain unclear, but they apparently ranged from the political to the strategic. Relevant factors included the orientation of India's new government, the end of the Cold War and the dilution of New Delhi's ties with Moscow, concerns over China and its conventional and nuclear forces, and India's desire to be treated as a great power. Many people in India have never accepted the post–World War II order in which India is excluded from formal nuclear weapons status and permanent U.N. Security Council membership whereas China and others are not. In the wake of India's test, Pakistan's decision to follow suit was more predictable and was also a result of political and strategic calculations.

Whatever the cause or causes of either country's actions, it is the Task Force's view that the Indian and Pakistani nuclear tests

---

[2] Ibid., p. 4.

have made South Asia and the world a more dangerous place. The presence of nuclear forces in the arsenals of two adjacent and often quarreling countries increases the likelihood that nuclear weapons could be used in a conflict—and dramatically raises the human and financial costs of any armed confrontation should deterrence fail.

This assessment is not universally shared. There is a view that nuclear deterrence contributed to stability between the United States and the Soviet Union during the Cold War—and that it could do the same for India and Pakistan today. This is possible but hardly likely. Deterrence between the United States and the Soviet Union was often fragile and came close to breaking down on more than one occasion. It took decades for the two countries to build robust capabilities that provided a clear picture of the other side's forces, promoted control against unauthorized use, and promised sure and devastating retaliation even if the other side struck first. Moreover, the United States and the U.S.S.R. enjoyed certain advantages. They were far apart, with no border or directly contested issue separating them, and tacitly embraced rules of the road that discouraged direct military confrontation.

In contrast, India and Pakistan are neighbors, disputing both a border and the status of Kashmir. There is a history of armed conflict between them. Neither side possesses the accurate intelligence and warning systems or assured second-strike capabilities that constitute the bedrock of deterrence. As a result, the possibility of a nuclear conflict in South Asia, whether by design or accident, cannot be ruled out. No one should be sanguine about the prospects for regional stability.

U.S. efforts to prevent the current situation from coming about—a policy predicated on endeavoring to develop bilateral ties with both India and Pakistan and deterring nuclear proliferation through (among other actions) the threat of comprehensive economic sanctions—may have slowed the advance of the two nuclear programs. But U.S. policy failed in the aftermath of the election of the new Indian government. Subsequent efforts by the Clinton administration to persuade Pakistan not to test by offering a set of inducements also failed.

Still, it is important to recall that even before these tests were carried out, both countries were known to have a threshold nuclear weapons capability and that India had once detonated a device. Moreover, there are several scenarios that can be imagined from this point on that would be far worse for South Asia and the world than the testing that has occurred. These include the actual deployment of nuclear weapons, an escalating nuclear arms race, the use of nuclear weapons, and the transfer of nuclear technology and materials to third parties. This is not to suggest that the recent testing of nuclear devices need lead inevitably to these even more destabilizing developments. Rather, it is precisely because the situation in South Asia could deteriorate with such terrible consequences that it must become a priority of post–Cold War American foreign policy to see that it does not.

THINKING THROUGH THE U.S. RESPONSE

In the wake of the nuclear tests, it is necessary as well not to lose sight of a critical fact, namely, that the United States has important interests in both India and Pakistan in addition to discouraging further nuclear proliferation in the region and any transfer of nuclear or missile technology to other parts of the world. These regional interests include preventing war of any sort in South Asia; promoting democracy and internal stability; expanding economic growth, trade, and investment; and developing political and, where applicable, military cooperation on a host of regional and global challenges, including but not limited to those posed by terrorism, drug trafficking, and environmental degradation. Both India and Pakistan are potential strategic partners of the United States as it seeks to shape the post–Cold War world. At least in principle, there is a potentially symbiotic relationship in all this: Closer American ties with India and Pakistan should buttress efforts to discourage further proliferation, while progress in containing a nuclear arms race will facilitate closer bilateral cooperation between both countries and the United States.

U.S. foreign policy should not sacrifice its many interests in South Asia in order to promote unrealistic aims in the nuclear realm. In particular, a complete "rollback" to a nonnuclear South Asia is simply not a realistic near- or even medium-term policy option for the United States. What India and Pakistan learned from the recent tests cannot be unlearned. For the foreseeable future, neither country will eliminate its stockpile of fissionable material or declare itself ready to sign the Nuclear Nonproliferation Treaty (NPT) as a nonnuclear weapons state. Policy departures of this magnitude are likely to be possible only in the context of unprecedented strides toward global nuclear disarmament and fundamental changes for the better in both Indo-Pakistan and Sino-Indian relations.

Unfortunately, U.S. policy—the introduction of broad economic sanctions for an indefinite period as called for by the Symington, Pressler, and Glenn amendments—is almost certain to make the challenge of promoting the full range of American interests more difficult.[3] That U.S. economic interests will suffer is obvious and needs no elaboration. But it is also likely that other interests—including the strengthening of democracy in Pakistan and the promotion of responsible behavior by both India and Pakistan in the nuclear realm—will also be adversely affected. The unintended consequences of U.S. sanctions are particularly pertinent to Pakistan, which is far more dependent than is India on international assistance. Sanctions could actually weaken political authority in Pakistan, a state already burdened by political, social, and economic problems, including massive foreign debt and negligible foreign exchange reserves. A stable Pakistan in possession of nuclear weapons is reason enough to worry; an unstable Pakistan would be that much worse. This consideration alone argues for rethinking current sanctions—and for working with Pakistan to implement long-overdue economic reform.

---

[3] For details, see the Appendix in this Task Force Report, "The Pressler, Symington, and Glenn Amendments" for the text of relevant legislation and "Fact Sheet: India and Pakistan Sanctions" for the administration's description of how sanctions are to be interpreted and implemented.

Advocates of punitive sanctions argue that the tests pose a major challenge to the global nonproliferation regime—even though neither India nor Pakistan is a party to the NPT or has signed the Comprehensive Test Ban Treaty (CTBT)—and that it is important that India and Pakistan be seen to suffer lest other countries conclude that they can follow suit with impunity. Although it is important that India and Pakistan be seen as paying a price (and certainly not be seen as being rewarded) for their decision to test, relying on broad-based economic sanctions for this purpose makes for questionable policy. As already noted, sanctions can work against U.S. interests, including the goal of promoting regional stability. Also, India and Pakistan will pay a price for what they have done apart from the sanctions. Beyond living with an increased risk of catastrophic conflict, both societies will have to bear the large financial burden of maintaining nuclear capabilities, especially if they decide to develop secure arsenals. Full-fledged nuclear programs—programs that include the intelligence, delivery systems, and communications support needed for robust deterrence—tend to be terribly expensive.[4] The tests and the resulting uncertainties will further detract from economic growth by discouraging foreign investment. There will be a political price to pay as well. India cannot have any hope of attaining U.N. Security Council membership any time soon; more generally, both countries will learn that possessing nuclear weapons and being a great power are two very different things.

Just as important for U.S. interests, there is no reason that a realistic policy toward India and Pakistan need encourage proliferation elsewhere. The United States has other tools at its disposal to employ on a case-by-case basis in the effort to frustrate proliferation. These include security commitments; the provision of conventional arms; diplomacy that reduces or eliminates the source of conflict; sanctions; economic incentives; export controls and supplier groups; a stronger International Atomic Energy Agency (IAEA); covert operations; preventive military strikes; and

---

[4] This was the conclusion of a recent study of the U.S. nuclear program. See Stephen I. Schwartz, editor, *Atomic Audit: The Costs and Consequences of U.S. Nuclear Weapons Since 1940* (Washington, D.C.: Brookings Institution, 1998).

arms control accords that limit the inventories and capabilities of the existing nuclear weapons states and reduce their reliance on nuclear weapons. Again, there is no necessary inconsistency between the goals of stabilizing South Asia and not fueling proliferation pressures elsewhere. Indeed, the United States has implemented a differentiated nonproliferation policy for over 40 years now with considerable success.

A COURSE OF ACTION

Consistent with the above, the immediate objective of U.S. foreign policy should be to encourage India and Pakistan to adopt policies that will help stabilize the situation in South Asia by capping their nuclear capabilities at their current levels and reinforcing the global effort to stem the horizontal and vertical proliferation of nuclear weapons and advanced delivery systems. Toward these ends, the Task Force calls upon India and Pakistan:

- to make a formal commitment to refrain from further nuclear weapons testing by signing the CTBT;

- to participate in good faith in negotiations that aim to end the production of fissile material and sign any Fissile Material Cut-Off Treaty (FMCT) that results;

- to announce a willingness to participate in a broad-based moratorium on producing fissile material;

- not to transfer nuclear or missile technology or equipment to any third party and to abide by Missile Technology Control Regime (MTCR) guidelines[5];

- not to deploy missiles with nuclear warheads or aircraft with nuclear bombs;

---

[5] Formed in 1987 by the Group of Seven leading industrial countries, the MTCR was originally designed to restrict the proliferation of nuclear-capable missiles and missile technology. Now consisting of over two dozen member states and others who voluntarily agree to adhere to its guidelines, the MTCR restricts technology exports that could contribute to the proliferation of missiles capable of delivering any weapons of mass destruction.

⊙to implement fully and unconditionally existing bilateral confidence-building measures (CBMs), including regular use of hot lines and the provision of advance notification of military exercises;

⊘to negotiate and implement additional CBMs (including regular high-level bilateral meetings, increased trade and other exchanges), exchanges of observers at military exercises, and a ban on ballistic missile flight tests in the direction of one another's territory (a prolonged pause in missile flight tests of any kind would enhance confidence even more);

⊙to initiate political, economic, and military steps designed to calm the situation in Kashmir while avoiding unilateral acts that could exacerbate tensions there; and

⊘to enter into sustained, serious negotiations with each other on the entire range of issues that divide them. Temporary positive action, followed by a reversion to enmity as has repeatedly been the case in the past, has become too dangerous to be repeated in the new, nuclear environment.

The Task Force realizes that it may prove extremely difficult to persuade India and Pakistan to undertake all the steps listed above. That said, we believe that these undertakings are justified and should be promoted on their merits. They would contribute to Indian and Pakistani security and welfare and to an improvement in relations between the two countries and between each of them and the United States. Both governments should be discouraged from insisting on linkage, i.e., from conditioning their own willingness to take constructive action in one area on the other's taking a desired step in another. In addition, the Clinton administration should not present these undertakings to either India or Pakistan as a formal package to be negotiated. Any such explicit approach is likely to make it more difficult for India and Pakistan to decide to take these steps. A formal treaty-like arrangement would also require careful monitoring (along with judgments of compliance) and set the stage for a new diplomatic crisis and new sanctions every time India or Pakistan did something inconsistent with its terms. Nor, given the independence of Congress, should sanctions relief be suggested as a quid pro quo for either country adopting desirable policies—although the Clinton administration will derive greater leverage in its efforts to seek sanctions relief from Congress the more that undertakings such as those listed above are formalized and carried out by India and Pakistan.

The narrow justifications for waiving sanctions in the Symington and Pressler legislation and the absence of any waiver whatsoever in the Glenn amendment constitute an obstacle to effective diplomacy. As a result, the Task Force calls upon Congress to provide broad waiver authority to the president so that sanctions and incentives can be used to support rather than thwart U.S. diplomacy. In a context in which India and/or Pakistan is taking some of the steps outlined above and amid signs that sanctions are working against U.S. foreign policy goals, the executive branch should remove the bulk of the remaining Symington, Pressler, and Glenn sanctions, keeping in place only those measures that block the provision of technology, material, and equipment that has the potential to contribute to Indian and Pakistani missile and nuclear efforts. Economic aid provided by the World Bank and private loans should be allowed to go ahead. Selective easing of controls on dual-use technology exports is also warranted. Here and elsewhere, the United States needs to move away from the "light switch" approach central to the Glenn amendment and toward a more modulated use of sanctions as symbolized by a rheostat. It is essential that the United States avoid remaining in or placing itself again in the sort of situation it now finds itself in, namely, one in which it has few tools to influence the course of events. Congress has already suspended some of the sanctions, and there are signs that it is prepared to give the president the authority to waive more or even most of them. This trend is to be applauded; to make it last, however, will require that the administration explain its evolving policy and engage in genuine consultations with Congress on a regular basis.

The United States should consider providing intelligence and selective technology to India and Pakistan in support of specific

CBMs to dispel rumors or disprove false assessments that could stimulate "unnecessary" arms competition or unauthorized or accidental use of nuclear weapons. The United States also should make available technologies and information that would enhance the safety of existing civil power installations. Encouraging and supporting a diversification of energy production makes sense as well. Restraints on military training and education should be loosened, given the important role of both the Indian and Pakistani militaries. The U.S. government should also be prepared to consider requests for arms sales on a case-by-case basis. Any arms sale that goes forward, however, should be justified on the ground that it enhances regional stability or contributes to the ability of India and/or Pakistan to act in a manner that contributes to U.S. national security objectives in the post–Cold War world.

CALMING KASHMIR

Kashmir remains the most dangerous point of contention between India and Pakistan. It is the issue with the greatest potential to trigger a conventional or even nuclear war. That said, the dispute is not ripe for final resolution. It is not even ripe for mediation by the United States or anyone else. Consistent with these realities, diplomacy aimed at now resolving the permanent political status of Kashmir is bound to fail.

Instead, using public and private diplomacy, the United States should work to encourage India and Pakistan to:

- refrain from provocative public rhetoric;

- convene bilateral talks (as well as three-way talks involving Delhi, Islamabad, and those representatives of the inhabitants of Kashmir who are willing to eschew violence) devoted to discussing ways of calming the situation in Kashmir;

- accept an increase in the number of international observers on both sides of the Line of Control to monitor troop dispositions and to discourage any armed support for militants; and

- accept a thinning of Indian and Pakistani forces along the Line of Control.

In addition, India should be urged to:

- grant increased political and economic autonomy to the inhabitants of Kashmir;

- reduce the size of its forces stationed in Kashmir that carry out policing functions; and

- accept an increase in the number of international observers monitoring human rights conditions within Kashmir.

At the same time, Pakistan should be urged to:

- eschew any use of military force in or near Kashmir;

- provide no material support to insurgents operating in Kashmir; and

- deny safe haven to any Kashmiri insurgent group. Pakistan's willingness to forswear any and all support for armed resistance against India is likely to be a condition for India's taking the steps suggested above.

MAKING DIPLOMACY WORK

China bears some responsibility for the situation in South Asia, given its own nuclear and missile programs that concern India and the assistance it has provided over the years to Pakistan's nuclear and missile programs. It will be difficult, if not impossible, to stabilize the situation in South Asia without China's constructive participation. China has an incentive to act responsibly, as it has no interest in stimulating the growth of India's nuclear arsenal, in destabilizing the region, or in devoting massive resources to the continuing modernization of its own nuclear capability. U.S. policy should encourage China to adhere to the MTCR and all of its annexes; end all unsafeguarded nuclear cooperation with Pakistan; participate in FMCT negotiations and announce a willingness to join in a moratorium on fissile material production; separate nuclear warheads from missiles so as to "de-alert" its forces and thereby pose less of a threat to India; enter into CBMs with India that increase the transparency of one another's forces; and announce a willingness to cap its own strategic force levels now and to participate in future Strategic Arms Reduction Treaty (START) talks once these negotiations contemplate levels at which China's arsenal becomes relevant. India and China should both be encouraged to develop further their own bilateral relationship and explore steps that could be taken to bridge existing differences.

The United States should not introduce additional political sanctions against India and Pakistan. The president should go ahead with a trip to the region (tentatively planned for late 1998 or early 1999). Such a visit provides an opportunity to address the problems caused by the recent tests and to advance other U.S. interests in the region. The United States retains an interest in deepening and broadening both bilateral relationships—just as India and Pakistan do with their relationships to the United States. Making a presidential trip conditional on India's and/or Pakistan's taking certain steps risks forfeiting what presidential visits could accomplish now and in the future. At the same time, it is in the interest of no party that a trip by President Clinton be dominated by an attempt to negotiate a specific response to the nuclear tests and a corresponding reduction in U.S. sanctions. The sooner that India and Pakistan announce they are taking steps to promote regional stability the better.

The United States should not offer unilateral security assurances to either protagonist at this time. Such assurances have been a source of misunderstanding in the past, and it is not at all obvious that U.S. assurances today would be enough to prevent a crisis from materializing—but such assurances could be enough to draw the United States into a complicated and dangerous situation.

The United States should not propose or support reopening the NPT to admit either India or Pakistan as nuclear weapons states. This would not be feasible given the opposition of many nuclear and nonnuclear states alike. Nor would it be desirable, given the importance of not sending a message that those who embark on a nuclear weapons program will be rewarded.

The United States should not use the five permanent members of the U.N. Security Council (the P-5) as a means to promote publicly its South Asia policy.[6] This group is viewed (with some reason) in New Delhi as antagonistic, given that it represents both the nuclear "haves" under the NPT and the U.N. Security Council—two groups that India believes it ought to be invited to join. The P-5 also excludes Japan and other countries that have something to offer to diplomacy. The Group of Eight (G-8) and ad hoc groupings of states—including those states that have given up a potential or actual nuclear weapons capability—provide better vehicles for future diplomacy.[7] Other countries, most notably Russia, Japan, and members of the European Union (EU), should also be pressed to coordinate diplomatic efforts and support limited sanctions.

FATEFUL CHOICES

The principal differences between what this report recommends and current U.S. policy toward India and Pakistan stem from legislation that initiated with Congress—legislation that both emphasizes nuclear-related concerns to the near exclusion of all else and the broad use of comprehensive and often unilateral economic sanctions. Our differences with the still-unfolding policy of the administration appear to be much less significant, although we would favor a stronger push for authority to waive sanctions, a decision to proceed with a presidential visit, and greater public articulation of the fact that U.S. interests in South Asia include but are not limited to discouraging nuclear proliferation. In addition, the United States needs to commit more diplomatic and intelligence resources to this part of the world than has been the norm. The

---

[6] The five are China, France, Russia, the United Kingdom, and the United States.

[7] Membership in the G-8 includes Canada, France, Germany, Italy, Japan, Russia, the United Kingdom, and the United States. The European Union is also represented. Russia is a member for discussion of political issues, but not for economic issues discussed by finance ministers.

fact that India tested, and that this test caught U.S. policymakers by surprise, was as much a long-term policy failure as a near-term intelligence failure. U.S. interests in South Asia have been increasing for years; so, too, now are the threats to those interests. India has the potential to be a major power in Asia as the next century opens; Pakistan can have a significant impact in both Central Asia and the Gulf. U.S. foreign policy needs to reflect this altered reality and accord a higher priority to South Asia and to all those actors in and outside the region who are in a position to influence its future.

It is no less true that the course of U.S. foreign policy toward South Asia, and the future of India and Pakistan, will be affected significantly and possibly fundamentally by how well India and Pakistan manage their nuclear competition. The United States and others can play a useful role in this regard, but the critical choices can only be made by India and Pakistan; no outsider can "manage" South Asia's future for them. It is not too late for India and Pakistan to take steps to cap their nuclear programs and to improve their relationship with each other. The Task Force urges both countries to take advantage of such opportunities while they still exist.

ADDITIONAL AND DISSENTING VIEWS

ADDITIONAL VIEWS

The Co-Chairs are to be congratulated for forging a balanced and cogent report from the strong and diverse views of the Task Force members.

Great care is warranted, however, before loosening existing sanctions or restraints on sales of dual-use technology or weaponry to India and Pakistan. Past experience suggests that the sale of modern, high-technology armaments to these countries provides little if any nonproliferation leverage and risks worsening tensions between them. Dual-use technologies also remain subject to misuse and their transfers require great care.

Although sanctions are a blunt instrument, difficult to implement and sustain, they offered a vital means, stronger than words, to make clear American opposition to the May 1998 series of nuclear tests. This tool should not be lightly tossed aside, but, as the report stressed, needs to be carefully calibrated to nuclear ground truth in South Asia. In that regard, it would be counterproductive to weaken sanctions before either India or Pakistan has taken any of the steps the Task Force rightly considers essential to walking the subcontinent back from the nuclear brink. Not only would the United States appear to be rewarding proliferation, we would be weakening our ability to use sanctions as tools in several other crisis situations, such as Russian nuclear and missile sales to Iran, and Iraqi compliance with U.N. inspections.

This is true even in a situation where many of our allies have not implemented similar sanctions. Elliot Abrams recently noted in the *Weekly Standard,* "The argument against unilateral sanctions is an argument against American leadership and suggests that if we cannot get some sort of majority vote from other traders and investors, we must set our scruples aside." The larger issue, he says, "is whether foreign policy should be driven by commercial objectives or only informed by them." While some adjustments are need-ed to the sanctions we have imposed in this instance, the United States should avoid swinging the pendulum too far in the other direction.

Joseph Cirincione
Lewis A. Dunn

The Report of the Independent Task Force outlines a prudent and realistic approach to the issues raised by India's and Pakistan's deci-sions to explode nuclear devices. One can wish that the two countries had not taken the momentous decision to go forward toward adding nuclear weapons to their arsenals and to risk nuclearizing their mutual conflicts. Given what has occurred, however, and in view of the very real dangers presented, it is wise that the United States preserve the capacity to engage both states independently. Unless the president has the authority to waive and ultimately remove sanctions against both states, it will be impos-sible to provide the inducements and support necessary to address the vital security concerns that underlie both states' recent actions and thereby contribute effectively to regional and global securi-ty. The Task Force Report makes the considered, difficult, and ulti-mately necessary judgment that the U.S. interest in preserving regional security should be balanced with, rather than subordinated to, the large and substantial interests of the United States in pre-serving the credibility of the global nuclear nonproliferation regime.

Beyond the immediate security issues, the report also recalls and endorses the conclusion of a different, earlier Task Force Report that "the time is ripe for the United States to propose a closer strate-gic relationship with India, which has the potential to emerge as a full-fledged major power." This important emphasis on the longer-term strategic interests and opportunities presented by India is especially salutary in the present context, where short-term pressures obscure more fundamental developments and relation-ships. One important lesson of recent developments has been to remind us all that strategic dialogue with India requires that Indian security perceptions be understood in terms that are broader than the South Asian regional security and global nuclear nonproliferation settings.

Finally, the report makes the case for waiving or removing sanctions against both India and Pakistan on the narrowest ground of security. This is wise, since the case against using sanctions to achieve U.S. security goals is cogent on the merits. There is a danger, however, that the report could, through its silence, contribute to a one-sided view of the meaning of "strategic engagement." While American commercial interests are acknowledged, these are not elaborated in any detail. Nor does the report recognize the great potential importance of strong U.S. commercial relations with both states in supporting the strategic approach outlined in the report or in enhancing both nations' security. It is true that the prospect of reduced trade and investment ties with the United States has been an insufficient inducement to deter India and Pakistan from taking actions that they believe are necessary to their core security. It does not follow, however, that strategic engagement can proceed without a strong commercial underpinning. U.S. business relationships offer important secondary channels of communication, strengthen mutual understanding, and, most importantly, build broad foundations of common interest and trust. U.S. companies also provide an important bridge between India and Pakistan.

Strong commercial relations should not be viewed as an inducement to cooperation in the "strategic" realm of conventional and nuclear military balances, but should instead be seen as a vital and indispensable element of a well-crafted strategic approach. The important dialogue that has emerged between the U.S. business community and the administration in recent months should be further institutionalized, even as it is agreed that commercial relations with South Asia should be allowed to develop in ways that are largely independent of the state of political relations.

Michael T. Clark

As a practical political matter, the nuclear issue will dominate any near-term presidential visit to the region, no matter how much the parties concerned may officially insist that it does not. For this reason, the president should go ahead with a trip sometime in the next several months *only* if it is an integral part of a larger strategy to address the problems caused by the recent tests (as well as to advance other interests in the region), and only if enough progress has been made with both India and Pakistan that the nuclear issue does not become the major measure of its "success." In this latter regard, the administration will face a difficult choice if, as may be likely, progress with India on the nuclear issue substantially outpaces progress with Pakistan. In such an event, a decision will have to be made about whether nevertheless to proceed with a visit to Pakistan, or snub Pakistan and jeopardize important U.S. interests by driving an even deeper wedge between Washington and Islamabad.

Arnold Kanter

Several of the additional and dissenting views emphasize the imperative of not diminishing nonproliferation within the hierarchy of U.S. foreign policy interests and worry that the report may seem weak in this regard. I agree. However, distinctions need to be made. Nonproliferation generally means preventing the acquisition of nuclear weapon capabilities. With India and Pakistan, the challenge now is different: to prevent a nuclear and ballistic missile arms race and then later, hopefully, to achieve "unproliferation." High-level Indian and Pakistani leaders have said they wish to avoid an arms race. These intentions are genuine. Yet, unless things change, the cynicism of partisan politicians within each democracy, and the volatility of relations between them, will generate pressures for arms racing in an unending quest for national technological superiority and domestic political supremacy. The only way to avoid these dynamics is to achieve arms control agreements now, before the competition gets out of control. Agreements to ban fissile material production, limit missile numbers and deployments, and put other fences around the nuclear and missile establishments can spare

India and Pakistan the costs and dangers of arms racing. To the limited extent that the U.S. government can encourage and facilitate such arms control agreements, every effort should be made to do so. The onus, however, is on the political parties of Pakistan and India to show that they can rise above cynical office seeking to form a national and binational consensus in favor of arms control. The report focuses too little on the need for more responsible political leadership in India and Pakistan.

Conversely, when it comes to "unproliferation," or the undoing of nuclear and ballistic missile capabilities, the United States and the other four recognized nuclear weapons states will have to do more than the Task Force Report or the additional views acknowledge. To achieve nonproliferation or unproliferation, the recognized nuclear weapon states must make a clearer, genuine commitment to the goal of creating the conditions for the elimination of deployed nuclear arsenals worldwide. Strategic and security factors link India's (and therefore Pakistan's) nuclear policies to China's nuclear policies, and so on up the chain through Russia and the United States. But even stronger than these security linkages is the reality that unproliferation is a political act. In a proud, post-colonial democracy like India, the public and competing political parties demand equity in relations with peer states. India wants to be seen as a major-power peer of China, Russia, and the United States, not to mention Britain and France. Although India has not acquired the economic foundation of a truly major power, Britain's and France's statuses suggest mistakenly that nuclear capability could provide a short cut. Democratic India will not roll back its nuclear capabilities unless and until these states commit themselves genuinely to do the same.

The Task Force Report acknowledges the connection between progress in global denuclearization and roll back, but the point deserves greater prominence: U.S. national security objectives in reversing the spread of nuclear weapons and strengthening the global nonproliferation regime cannot be achieved without a clearer, more energetic effort to specify and create the conditions for the verifiable elimination of deployed nuclear weapons worldwide. Failure to do this will, over time, heighten the frustration of equity-seeking people and leaders in the large democracies, thereby undermining the global regime that the United States so effectively helped create in an era prior to the bloom of democratization in Asia, South America, and eastern Europe.

George Perkovich

While I believe the Task Force Report is largely on target in its analysis and recommendations, care needs to be taken to ensure that it is not misconstrued as a dilution or abandonment of U.S. nonproliferation goals.

Full achievement of those goals—including universal membership in the Nuclear Nonproliferation Treaty—will not come quickly, and pressing for them prematurely could be counterproductive. The report properly identifies more pragmatic, short-term goals. That said, abandoning more ambitious goals as a long-term objective in South Asia could aggravate proliferation problems far beyond that region in the years ahead. It is also worth emphasizing that, in South Asia as elsewhere, U.S. policy will be more effective in advancing our nonproliferation goals to the degree that we can secure multilateral support for any approach that we advocate.

Daniel Poneman

While I share many of the views expressed in the above report, there are certain aspects with which I do not agree. My primary concern is that as written, the report fails to give proper focus to long-standing nonproliferation principles, commitment, and policy. Rather, they are treated as somewhat secondary aspects of our policy. This is evident, for example, in the first paragraph in the section "Thinking Through the U.S. Response" in which primary emphasis is given to a range of interests the United States has in the region in addition to discouraging further nuclear proliferation. In my view, the priority objective should be to discourage any further proliferation activity without, in so doing, ignoring the fact that we do have other interests in South Asia. The point becomes clearer when looking at the following paragraph, which asserts that our foreign policy should "not sacrifice its many interests in South Asia in order to promote unrealistic aims in the nuclear realm." It is not difficult to envisage how policies predicated on this approach could result in damage to the principle of nonproliferation and undermine the decades-long objective we have maintained in preventing the further spread of nuclear weapons. The opening of "A Course of Action" puts us back on course with its list of actions that India and Pakistan should be called upon to agree and to implement.

The point in the next paragraph that both countries should be discouraged from seeking linkage between steps taken pursuant to calls from the G-8 and P-5 on negotiated deals with the United States is well taken but deserves to be stated even more forcefully—there can be no question of deals being struck on a tit-for-tat basis. Even more importantly, no step on our part should be countenanced that permits India to come away with the view that the path to great power recognition flows from behavior contrary to nearly universally shared norms and undertakings.

There is no need—and the potential exists for resulting damage—to suggest offering nuclear energy cooperation to India as suggested in the second paragraph of the report. U.S. civil nuclear power cooperation has long been predicated on acceptance by the receiving state of full-scope or comprehensive safeguards—a condition that all 181 nonnuclear weapons state parties to the Nonproliferation Treaty accept and which is now a fundamental aspect of the nuclear supplier regime that has been agreed to by virtually every nuclear supplier of consequence except China. To offer looser terms and conditions to India not only flies in the face of our own long-standing principles, laws, and policy, but can only work to undermine an important element of the nonproliferation regime. There is ample opportunity to cooperate with India in a range of areas including nonnuclear energy, which in fact may be an economically more sound investment in the near and midterm in any event.

Lawrence Scheinman

DISSENTING VIEWS

In the 1997 Council on Foreign Relations Task Force Report, my appended statement disagreed with several tenets of the report that would have downgraded the priority of American efforts to prevent further nuclear proliferation in the subcontinent. My addendum also urged that any validation of India's aspirations for major power status be conditioned on India's exercise of responsibility and restraint. In fact, India's May 1998 nuclear testing breakout, which inevitably triggered a nuclear response in kind from Pakistan, struck quite the opposite course, evidently seeking to coerce the foreign respect that India's national policies and behavior have failed to generate naturally. The current Indian government's willful damage to the goals of nonproliferation and international security will take years to fully assess and remedy. But there is little doubt that India's action attacks the existing nonproliferation regime—not only by supplying new models of diplomatic disingenuousness to those other states that are known to covet nuclear weapons anyway, but by raising doubts about the viability of nonproliferation in the thinking of strategically important, NPT-abiding states, such as Japan, that have until now firmly shunned nuclear weapons on the assumption that nuclear proliferation will neither flourish nor be allowed to destabilize regional balances of power. In this respect, the potential repercussions of India's nuclear breakout could be profoundly inimical to U.S. national as well as international security.

The current Task Force Report fails to address these issues meaningfully, in my view, and harbors a romantic vision that U.S. foreign policy goals toward South Asia will be served in the wake of the May 1998 nuclear detonations anyway—if we only move the goalpost a bit, and try a little harder to do what the previous report advocated. The task of devising a sophisticated strategy to deal with the array of problems in South Asia is indeed a difficult one. A meaningful report probably would require much deeper Task Force work and a more extended deliberation. Under the circumstances, I respectfully dissociate myself from the following points of view or conclusions of the current Task Force Report:

1. that "strategic partnership" is an appropriate term of reference for U.S. relations with South Asia in the post–Cold War environment;

2. that U.S. and multilateral restrictions on nuclear and sensitive dual-use technology transfer to India and Pakistan should be lifted (in the absence of binding nuclear nonproliferation regime gains equivalent to NPT adherence);

3. that failures of U.S. nonproliferation policy toward this region are due chiefly to sanctions legislation, and that sanctions invariably thwart, rather than facilitate, the diplomatic pursuit of U.S. interests in South Asia;

4. that proliferation in the subcontinent should be accommodated (or "managed") and that this will make it easier to contain the external repercussions;

5. that it is politically realistic to imagine that India and Pakistan will be willing or able, alone, to work out a constructive, durable resolution of the main disputes that alienate each from the other;

6. that it is right to use revenue from U.S. taxpayers to subsidize any government that has defied international nuclear nonproliferation norms for patently political ends (in the absence of serious external nuclear threat); and

7. that a U.S. presidential visit to South Asia so soon after India's and Pakistan's nuclear tests would benefit rather than undercut long-term U.S. objectives in the region (even if there is no advance assurance of binding nuclear nonproliferation and non-deployment commitments by India and Pakistan).

A brief note on peacetime use of sanctions for U.S. foreign policy and nonproliferation objectives: It is well to remember that nonproliferation sanctions are "peaceful" alternatives to the use of military instruments and force (including the classical use of arms supply and alliances to rectify military imbalances and blunt incentives to resort to war). To shrink the policy menu of peaceful alternatives by denigrating sanctions—at the risk of draining them of future credibility—is a quixotic enterprise. It is important to tally up the successes that have been accomplished over time by foreign reluctance to trigger nonproliferation sanctions, an assessment that has not been attempted in this Task Force. In the event that sanctions laws are misapplied or become ineffectual owing to altered circumstances, the appropriate response is not to throw the baby out with the bathwater but rather to reconfigure the sanctions for greater effectiveness. Even the report recognizes implicitly that the future U.S. diplomatic steps it recommends to stabilize Indo-Pakistani relations and their own bilateral actions to defuse confrontation will have little lasting value unless they are explicit and enforceable, that is, sanctionable.

Rodney Jones

The reasoning that undergirds this report is seriously flawed, even though many of the recommendations that flow from the report's questionable assumptions are commendable.

One of the report's basic assumptions is that sanctions are unhelpful instruments of U.S. national security policy. Another is that the United States has placed too much emphasis on nonproliferation in South Asia at the expense of other important objectives, such as economic engagement now hindered by the sanctions imposed after nuclear tests by India and Pakistan.

In my view, the high priority given to nonproliferation by Republican and Democratic leaders has been reaffirmed, not diminished, by the nuclear dangers now painfully evident in South Asia. Indeed, the possible damage to nonproliferation regimes resulting from nuclear tests, the slight testing of nuclear-capable missiles, and the storage of these missiles near launch sites in India and Pakistan is so great as to confirm the necessity of placing efforts to reduce nuclear dangers at the top of any list of U.S. national security policy objectives.

The damage to nonproliferation norms from recent developments in South Asia may not be limited to the subcontinent. Opportunistic acts of proliferation have already occurred elsewhere. The government of Iran has chosen to flight-test its new medium-range ballistic missile in the dark shadow of nuclear testing by India and Pakistan, just as North Korea has chosen this particular time to begin unfreezing its nuclear program. The subterranean proliferation partnerships are now becoming more visible and troubling. This report argues that the United States can respond generously to nuclear dangers in South Asia without impacting adversely on nonproliferation objectives in other regions. I wish this assertion were true, but U.S. policy cannot be based on such hopes. While every act of proliferation is grounded in singular circumstances, external responses help to shape subsequent steps.

This report also suggests that U.S. sanctions are a major impediment to realizing the full panoply of U.S. objectives in South Asia. Congressionally mandated sanctions, however, have already been greatly modulated. Moreover, no flows of private capital have been prohibited by these sanctions. Instead capital flows have been greatly diminished due to the poor performance of the Pakistani and Indian economies, bureaucratic and political constraints, corrupt practices, as well as the concerns of investors about the nuclear dangers and regional instabilities generated by recent developments. In addition, the United States has not opposed the provision of World Bank loans for humanitarian purposes.

U.S. imposed sanctions are not the cause of the difficulties now facing India and Pakistan, which are primarily domestic in origin. Nor have these sanctions appreciably restrained noneconomic forms of U.S. engagement with South Asia. Nonetheless, U.S. sanctions can continue to exacerbate indigenous problems. I agree with this report's conclusion that the United States can and should lift sanctions—except in the sensitive areas noted—but must somehow do so in ways that do not damage further global efforts to reduce nuclear dangers. This is far from a simple task.

The Task Force's endorsement of a "rheostat" approach to sanctions' relief can be helpful in this regard. Congress would be wise to provide the executive branch with sufficient leeway to respond proportionately and favorably to concrete steps taken by either India or Pakistan (or preferably, both countries acting in concert) to reduce the nuclear dangers they have unleashed. The president also requires the leeway to respond proportionately and negatively to new steps that increase nuclear dangers. Neither country should be held hostage under U.S. law to the recalcitrance of its neighbor.

In this as well as the previous report, I strongly object to the recommendation that the United States should consider selective arms transfers to India and Pakistan on a case-by-case basis. Such transfers should be approved only in the event of irreversible progress toward reconciliation on the subcontinent, or in the event that either country faces a serious external threat.

Lastly, this report recommends without qualification that the president visit South Asia this fall. I can foresee circumstances in which such a visit could impact negatively on U.S. relations with both countries, nonproliferation norms, as well as on domestic political developments in India and Pakistan. All of these considerations warrant very careful deliberation before endorsing additional presidential travel this fall.

Michael Krepon

MEMBERS OF THE TASK FORCE

RICHARD K. BETTS is Professor of Political Science and Director of the Institute of War and Peace Studies at Columbia University. He is also a Senior Fellow at the Council on Foreign Relations.

BRUCE BLAIR is a Senior Fellow in the Foreign Policy Studies program at the Brookings Institution. He served as a launch officer in the Strategic Air Command and as a nuclear weapons and control specialist for the Defense Department and the Congressional Office of Technology Assessment.

MARSHALL M. BOUTON is Executive Vice President of the Asia Society. He has served in State and Defense Department positions dealing with South Asia and is author of "India's Problem Is Not Politics" in *Foreign Affairs* (May/June 1998).

JOSEPH CIRINCIONE* is a Senior Associate and Director of the Non-Proliferation Project at the Carnegie Endowment for International Peace. He served for nine years on the professional staff of the House Committee on Armed Services and the Committee on Governmental Operations.

MICHAEL T. CLARK* is Executive Director of the U.S.-India Business Council. He has held a variety of positions at the intersections of policy and academia, and was most recently Reves Scholar in Residence at the college of William and Mary (1993–97).

STEPHEN P. COHEN formerly of the University of Illinois, is Senior Research Fellow in the Foreign Policy Studies program at the

---

Note: Institutional affiliations are for identification purposes only.
*Individual has submitted an additional view.
†Individual has submitted a dissenting view.

[27]

Brookings Institution. He was a visiting scholar with the Ford Foundation in India, served two years in the Policy Planning Staff of the Department of State, and is the author of several books on South Asian security issues.

LEWIS A. DUNN* is a Corporate Vice President of Science Applications International Corporation (SAIC) and Director of SAIC's Center for Global Security and Cooperation. He is a former Assistant Director of the U.S. Arms Control and Disarmament Agency and Ambassador for Non-Proliferation Treaty matters.

FRANCINE R. FRANKEL is Director of the Center for the Advanced Study of India and Professor of Political Science at the University of Pennsylvania. She is the author or contributing editor of five books on India and spent 1997–98 at the Woodrow Wilson Center for International Scholars writing a book on elite perceptions and foreign policymaking in the United States and India.

SUMIT GANGULY is Professor of Political Science at Hunter College of the City University of New York. He is the author of *The Crisis in Kashmir: Portents of War, Hopes of Peace.*

RICHARD N. HAASS is Director of Foreign Policy Studies at the Brookings Institution. He was Senior Director for Near East and South Asian Affairs on the National Security Council staff during the Bush administration.

MORTON H. HALPERIN is Senior Vice President of The Century Foundation. He is also a Senior Fellow at the Council on Foreign Relations and a former official of the National Security Council and the Department of Defense.

NEIL JOECK is a political analyst at the Lawrence Livermore National Laboratory. His most recent publication is "Maintaining Nuclear Stability in South Asia," *Adelphi Paper 312*, which he wrote as a Research Associate at the International Institute for Strategic Studies, London.

RODNEY W. JONES[†] is President of Policy Architects International and coauthor of the new book *Tracking Nuclear Proliferation*. He is a former official of the Arms Control and Disarmament Agency.

ARNOLD KANTER[*] is a Senior Fellow at the Forum for International Policy. He served in the Bush administration as Undersecretary of State for Political Affairs and as Special Assistant to the President for Defense Policy and Arms Control.

GEOFFREY KEMP is Director of Regional Strategic Programs at the Nixon Center. He served in the White House during the first Reagan administration and was Special Assistant to the President for National Security Affairs and Senior Director for Near East and South Asian Affairs on the National Security Council staff.

MICHAEL KREPON[†] is President of the Henry L. Stimson Center and coeditor of *Crisis Prevention, Confidence-Building and Reconciliation in South Asia*.

ROBERT A. MANNING is Senior Fellow and Director of Asian Studies at the Council on Foreign Relations. He served as Adviser for Asia Policy at the Department of State from 1989 to 1993.

ROBERT B. OAKLEY is a retired Foreign Service Officer who served as Ambassador to Pakistan and on the National Security Council staff as Assistant to the President for the Middle East and South Asia.

GEORGE PERKOVICH[*] is Deputy Director for Programs and Director of the Secure World Program at the W. Alton Jones Foundation. He is the author of the forthcoming book *India's Nuclear Bomb*.

Note: Institutional affiliations are for identification purposes only.
[*]Individual has submitted an additional view.
[†]Individual has submitted a dissenting view.

DANIEL B. PONEMAN,* formerly Special Assistant to the President and Senior Director for Nonproliferation and Export Controls, served on the National Security Council staff from 1990 to 1996. He is currently a partner at the law firm of Hogan & Hartson in Washington, D.C.

GIDEON ROSE is Deputy Director of National Security Studies and Olin Fellow at the Council on Foreign Relations. From 1994 to 1995, he served as Associate Director for Near East and South Asian Affairs on the National Security Council staff.

LAWRENCE SCHEINMAN* is Distinguished Professor of Public Policy and Director of the Washington Office of the Monterey Institute of International Studies and former Assistant Director of the U.S. Arms Control and Disarmament Agency.

GORDON R. SULLIVAN is a retired General of the U.S. Army and a member of the Council on Foreign Relations.

FRANK G. WISNER serves as Vice Chairman for External Affairs at the American International Group. From 1994 to 1997, he served as U.S. Ambassador to India.

Note: Institutional affiliations are for identification purposes only.
*Individual has submitted an additional view.
†Individual has submitted a dissenting view.

Appendixes

Appendixes

THE PRESSLER, SYMINGTON, AND GLENN AMENDMENTS

Nuclear Proliferation Prevention Act of 1994
(Amends Arms Export Control Act)

International Security and Development
Cooperation Act of 1985

Sec. 902. Nuclear Non-Proliferation Conditions on Assistance
for Pakistan (Pressler Amendment)

Section 620E of the Foreign Assistance Act of 1961 is amended by adding at the end thereof the following new subsection:

"(e) No assistance shall be furnished to Pakistan and no military equipment or technology shall be sold or transferred to Pakistan, pursuant to the authorities contained in this Act or any other Act, unless the President shall have certified in writing to the Speaker of the House of Representatives and the chairman of the Committee on Foreign Relations of the Senate, during the fiscal year in which assistance is to be furnished or military equipment or technology is to be sold or transferred, that Pakistan does not possess a nuclear explosive device and that the proposed United States assistance program will reduce significantly the risk that Pakistan will possess a nuclear explosive device."

Sec. 101. Nuclear Enrichment Transfers
(Symington Amendment)

(A) Prohibitions; Safeguards and Management.

Except as provided in subsection (B) of this section, no funds made available to carry out the Foreign Assistance Act of 1961 or this Act may be used for the purpose of providing economic assistance (including assistance under chapter 4 of part II of the Foreign Assistance Act of 1961), providing military assistance or grant military education and training, providing assistance under

[33]

chapter 6 of part II of that Act, or extending military credits or making guarantees, to any country which the President determines delivers nuclear enrichment equipment, materials, or technology to any other country on or after August 4, 1977, or receives such equipment, materials, or technology from any country on or after August 4, 1977, unless before such delivery:

(1) the supplying country and receiving country have reached agreement to place all such equipment, materials, or technology, upon delivery, under multilateral auspices and management when available; and

(2) the recipient country has entered into an agreement with the International Atomic Energy Agency to place all such equipment, materials, technology, and all nuclear fuel and facilities in such country under the safeguards system of such Agency.

(B) Certification by President of Necessity of Continued Assistance; Disapproval by Congress.

(1) Notwithstanding subsection (a) of this section, the President may furnish assistance which would otherwise be prohibited under such subsection if he determines and certifies in writing to the Speaker of the House of Representatives and the Committee on Foreign Relations of the Senate that (a) the termination of such assistance would have a serious adverse effect on vital United States interests; and

(b) he has received reliable assurances that the country in question will not acquire or develop nuclear weapons or assist other nations in doing so.

Such certification shall set forth the reasons supporting such determination in each particular case.

(2)(a) A certification under paragraph (1) of this subsection shall take effect on the date on which the certification is received by the Congress. However, if, within thirty calendar days after receiving this certification, the Congress enacts a joint resolution stating in substance that the Congress disapproves the furnishing of assistance pursuant to the certification, then upon the enactment of that resolution the certification shall cease to be effective and all deliveries of assistance furnished under the authority of that certification shall be suspended immediately.

(b) Any joint resolution under this paragraph shall be considered in the Senate in accordance with the provisions of section 601(b) of the International Security Assistance and Arms Export Control Act of 1976.

Sec. 102. Nuclear Reprocessing Transfers, Illegal Exports for Nuclear Explosive Devices, Transfers of Nuclear Explosive Devices, and Nuclear Detonations (Glenn Amendment)

(A) Prohibitions on Assistance to Countries Involved in Transfer of Nuclear Reprocessing Equipment, Materials, or Technology; Exceptions, Procedures Applicable

(1) Except as provided in paragraph (2) of this subsection, no funds made available to carry out the Foreign Assistance Act of 1961 or this Act may be used for the purpose of providing economic assistance (Including assistance under chapter 4 of part II of the Foreign Assistance Act of 1961), providing military assistance or grant military education and training, providing assistance under chapter 6 or part II of that Act, or extending military credits or making guarantees, to any country which the President determines—

(a) delivers nuclear reprocessing equipment, materials, or technology to any other country on or after August 4, 1977, or receives such equipment, materials, or technology from any other country on or after August 4, 1977 (except for the transfer of reprocessing technology associated with the investigation, under international evaluation programs in which the United States participates, of technologies which are alternatives to pure plutonium reprocessing), or

(b) is a non-nuclear-weapon state which, on or after August 8, 1985, exports illegally (or attempts to export illegally) from the United States any materials, equipment, or technology which would contribute significantly to the ability of such country to manufacture a nuclear explosive device, if the President determines that the material, equipment, or technology was to be used by such country in the manufacture of a nuclear explosive device.

For the purposes of clause (B), an export (or attempted export) by a person who is an agent of, or is otherwise acting on behalf of or in the interest of, a country shall be considered to be an export (or attempted export) by that country.

(2) Notwithstanding paragraph (1) of this subsection, the President in any fiscal year may furnish assistance which would otherwise be prohibited under that paragraph if he determines and certifies in writing during that fiscal year to the Speaker of the House of Representatives and to the Chairman of the Committee on Foreign Relations of the Senate that the termination of such assistance would be seriously prejudicial to the achievement of the United States non-proliferation objectives or otherwise jeopardize the common defense and security. The President shall transmit with such certification a statement setting forth the specific reasons therefor.

(3)(a) A certification under paragraph (2) of this subsection shall take effect on the date on which the certification is received by the Congress. However, if, within 30 calendar days after receiving this certification, the Congress enacts a joint resolution stating in substance that the Congress disapproves the furnishing of assistance pursuant to the certification, then upon the enactment of that resolution the certification shall cease to be effective and all deliveries of assistance furnished under the authority of that certification shall be suspended immediately.

(b) Any joint resolution under this paragraph shall be considered in the Senate in accordance with the provision of section 601(b) of the International Security Assistance and Arms Export Control Act of 1976.

(B) Prohibitions on Assistance to Countries Involved in Transfer or Use of Nuclear Explosive Devices; Exceptions; Procedures Applicable: (1) Except as provided in paragraphs (4), (5), and (6), in the event that the President determines that any country, after the effective date of part B of the Nuclear Proliferation Prevention Act of 1994.

(a) transfers to a non-nuclear-weapon state a nuclear explosive device,

(b) is a non-nuclear-weapon state and either:

(i) receives a nuclear explosive device, or

(ii) detonates a nuclear explosive device,

(c) transfers to a non-nuclear-weapon state any design information or component which is determined by the President to be important to, and known by the transferring country to be intended by the recipient states for use in, the development or manufacture of any nuclear explosive devices, or (d) is a non-nuclear-weapon state and seeks and receives any design information or component which is determined by the President to be important to, and intended by the recipient states for use in, the development or manufacture of any nuclear explosive device, then the President shall forthwith report in writing his determination to the Congress and shall forthwith impose the sanctions described in paragraph (2) against that country.

(2) The sanctions referred to in paragraph (1) are as follows:

(a) The United States Government shall terminate assistance to that country under the Foreign Assistance Act of 1961, except for humanitarian assistance or food or other agricultural commodities.

(b) The United States Government shall terminate:

(i) sales to that country under this Act of any defense articles, defense services, or design and construction services and

(ii) licenses for the export to that country of any item on the United States Munitions List.

(c) The United States Government shall terminate all foreign military assistance for that country under this Act.

(d) The United States Government shall deny to that country any credit, credit guarantees, or other financial assistance by any department, agency, or instrumentality of the United States Government, except that the sanction of this subparagraph shall not apply:

(i) to any transaction subject to the reporting requirements of title V of the National Security Act of 1947 (relating to congressional oversight of intelligence activities), or

(ii) to humanitarian assistance.

(e) The United States Government shall oppose, in accordance with section 701 of the International Financial Institutions Act (22 U.S.C. 262d), the extension of any loan or financial or technical assistance to that country by an international financial institution.

(f) The United States Government shall prohibit any United States bank from making any loan or providing any credit to the government of that country, except for loans or credits for the purpose of purchasing food or other agricultural commodities.

(g) The authorities of section 6 of the Export Administration Act of 1979 shall be used to prohibit exports to that country of specific goods and technology (excluding food and other agricultural commodities), except that such prohibition shall not apply to any transaction subject to the reporting requirements of title V of the National Security Act of 1947 (relating to congressional oversight of intelligence activities).

(3) As used in this subsection:

(a) the term 'design information' means specific information that relates to the design of a nuclear explosive device and that is not available to the public; and

(b) the term 'component' means a specific component of a nuclear explosive device.

(4)(a) Notwithstanding paragraph (1) of this subsection, the President may, for a period of not more than 30 days of continuous session, delay the imposition of sanctions which would otherwise be required under paragraph (1)(a) or (1)(b) of this subsection if the President first transmits to the Speaker of the House of Representatives, and to the chairman of the Committee on Foreign Relations of the Senate, a certification that he has determined that an immediate imposition of sanctions on that country would be detrimental to the national security of the United States. Not more than one such certification may be transmitted for a country with respect to the same detonation, transfer, or receipt of a nuclear explosive device.

(b) If the President transmits a certification to the Congress under subparagraph (a), a joint resolution which would permit the President to exercise the waiver authority of paragraph (5) of this subsection shall, if introduced in either House within thirty days of continuous session after the Congress receives this certification, be considered in the Senate in accordance with subparagraph 2 of this paragraph.

(c) Any joint resolution under this paragraph shall be considered in the Senate in accordance with the provisions of section 601(b) of the International Security Assistance and Arms Export Control Act of 1976.

(d) For purposes of this paragraph, the term 'joint resolution' means a joint resolution of the matter after the resolving clauses of which is as follows: "That the Congress having received on a _____ certification by the President under section 102(b)(4) of the Arms Export Control Act with respect to _____ the Congress hereby authorizes the President to exercise the waiver authority contained in section 102(b)(5) of that Act," with the date of receipt of the certification inserted in the first blank and the name of the country inserted in the second blank.

(5) Notwithstanding paragraph (1) of this subsection, if the Congress enacts a joint resolution under paragraph (4) of this subsection, the President may waive any sanction which would otherwise be required under paragraph (1)(a) or (1)(b) if he determined and certifies in writing to the Speaker of the House of Representatives and the chairman of the Committee on Foreign Relations of the Senate that the imposition of such sanction would be seriously prejudicial to the achievement of United States non-proliferation objectives or otherwise jeopardize the common defense and security. The President shall transmit with such certification a statement setting forth the specific reasons therefor.

(6)(a) In the event the President is required to impose sanctions against a country under paragraph (1)(c) or (1)(d), the President shall forthwith so inform such country and shall impose the required sanction beginning 30 days after submitting to the Congress the report required by paragraph (1) unless, and to the extent that, there is enacted during the 30-day period a law prohibiting the imposition of such sanctions.

(b) Notwithstanding any other provision of law, the sanctions which are required to be imposed against a country under paragraph (1)(c) or (1)(d) shall not apply if the President determines the certifies in writing to the Committee on Foreign Relations of the Senate and the Committee on Governmental Affairs of the House of Representatives that the application of such sanctions against a country would have a serious adverse effect on vital

United States interests. The President shall transmit with such certification a statement setting forth the specific reasons therefor.

(7) For the purposes of this subsection, continuity of session is
broken only by an adjournment of Congress sine die and the
days on which either House is not in session because of an
adjournment of more than three days to a day certain are excluded in the computation of any period of time in which Congress
is in continuous session.

(8) The President may not delegate or transfer his power,
authority, or discretion to make or modify determinations under
this subsection.

(C) Non-Nuclear-Weapon States defined. As used in this section,
the term 'non-nuclear-weapon state' means any country which is
not a nuclear-weapon state, as defined in Article IX(3) of the Treaty
on Non-Proliferation of Nuclear Weapons.

PAPER LAID ON THE TABLE OF INDIA'S LOWER HOUSE OF PARLIAMENT (LOK SABHA) ON EVOLUTION OF INDIA'S NUCLEAR POLICY

May 27, 1998

On 11 May a statement was issued by the Government announcing that India had successfully carried out three underground nuclear tests at the Pokhran range. Two days later, after carrying out two more underground sub-kiloton tests, the Government announced the completion of the planned series of tests. The three underground nuclear tests carried out at 1545 hours on 11 May were with three different devices—a fission device, a low-yield sub-kiloton device and a thermonuclear device. The two tests carried out at 1221 hours on 13 May were also low-yield devices in the sub-kiloton range. The results from these tests have been in accordance with the expectations of our scientists.

In 1947, when India emerged as a free country to take its rightful place in the comity of nations, the nuclear age had already dawned. Our leaders then took the crucial decision to opt for self-reliance, and freedom of thought and action. We rejected the Cold War paradigm whose shadows were already appearing on the horizon and instead of aligning ourselves with either bloc, chose the more difficult path of non-alignment. This has required the building up of national strength through our own resources, our skills and creativity and the dedication of the people. Among the earliest initiatives taken by our first Prime Minister, Pt. Jawaharlal Nehru, was the development of science and inculcation of the scientific spirit. It is this initiative that laid the foundation for the achievement of 11 and 13 May, made possible by exemplary cooperation among the scientists from the Department of Atomic Energy and Defence Research & Development Organisation. Disarmament was then and continues to be a major plank in our foreign policy now. It was, in essence, and remains still, the natural course for a country that had waged a unique struggle for independence on the basis of 'ahimsa' and 'satyagraha.'

Development of nuclear technology transformed the nature of global security. Our leaders reasoned that nuclear weapons were not weapons of war, these were weapons of mass destruction. A nuclear-weapon-free world would, therefore, enhance not only India's security but also the security of all nations. This is the principal plank of our nuclear policy. In the absence of universal and non-discriminatory disarmament, we cannot accept a regime that creates an arbitrary division between nuclear haves and have-nots. India believes that it is the sovereign right of every nation to make a judgement regarding its supreme national interests and exercise its sovereign choice. We subscribe to the principle of equal and legitimate security interests of nations and consider it a sovereign right. At the same time, our leaders recognised early that nuclear technology offers tremendous potential for economic development, especially for developing countries who are endeavouring to leap across the technology gaps created by long years of colonial exploitation. This thinking was reflected in the enactment of the Atomic Energy Act of 1948, within a year of our independence. All the numerous initiatives taken by us since, in the field of nuclear disarmament have been in harmony and in continuation of those early enunciations.

In the 50's, nuclear weapons testing took place above ground and the characteristic mushroom cloud became the visible symbol of the nuclear age. India then took the lead in calling for an end to all nuclear weapon testing as the first step for ending the nuclear arms race. Addressing the Lok Sabha on 2 April, 1954, shortly after a major hydrogen bomb test had been conducted, Pt. Jawaharlal Nehru stated that "nuclear, chemical and biological energy and power should not be used to forge weapons of mass destruction." He called for negotiations for prohibition and elimination of nuclear weapons and in the interim, a standstill agreement to halt nuclear testing. The world had by then witnessed less than 65 tests. Our call was not heeded. In 1963, an agreement was concluded to ban atmospheric testing but by this time, countries had developed the technologies for conducting underground nuclear tests and the nuclear arms race continued unabated. More than three decades passed and after over 2000 tests had been conducted, a Comprehensive Test Ban Treaty was opened for signature in 1996, following two and a half years of negotiations in which India had participated actively. In its final shape, this Treaty left much to be desired. It was neither comprehensive nor was it related to disarmament.

In 1965, along with a small group of non-aligned countries, India had put forward the idea of an international non-proliferation agreement under which the nuclear weapon states would agree to give up their arsenals provided other countries refrained from developing or acquiring such weapons. This balance of rights and obligations was absent when the Nuclear Non-Proliferation Treaty (NPT) emerged in 1968, almost 30 years ago. In the 60's our security concerns deepened. But such was our abhorrence of nuclear weapons and such our desire to avoid acquiring them that we sought instead security guarantees from major nuclear powers of the world. The countries we turned to for support and understanding felt unable to extend to us the assurances that we then sought. That is when and why India made clear its inability to sign the NPT.

The Lok Sabha debated the NPT on 5 April 1968. The then Prime Minister, late Smt. Indira Gandhi, assured the House that "we shall be guided entirely by our self-enlightenment and the considerations of national security." She highlighted the shortcomings of the NPT whilst reemphasising the country's commitment to nuclear disarmament. She warned the House and the country "that not signing the Treaty may bring the nation many difficulties. It may mean the stoppage of aid and stoppage of help. Since we are taking this decision together, we must all be together in facing its consequences." That was a turning point. This House then strengthened the decision of the Government by reflecting a national consensus.

Our decision not to sign the NPT was in keeping with the basic objective of maintaining freedom of thought and action. In 1974, we demonstrated our nuclear capability. Successive Governments thereafter have continued to take all necessary steps in keeping with that resolve and national will, to safeguard India's nuclear option. This was also the primary reason underlying the 1996 decision in the country not subscribing to the Comprehensive Test Ban Treaty (CTBT); a decision that met the unanimous approval of the House yet again. Our perception then was that subscribing to the CTBT would severely limit India's nuclear potential at an unacceptably low level. Our reservations deepened as the CTBT did not also carry forward the nuclear disarmament process. On both counts, therefore, yet again our security concerns remained unaddressed. The then Minister for External Affairs, Shri I. K. Gujral, had made clear the Government's reasoning to this House during the discussions on this subject in 1996.

The decades of the 80's and 90's meanwhile witnessed the gradual deterioration of our security environment as a result of nuclear and missile proliferation. In our neighbourhood, nuclear weapons increased and more sophisticated delivery systems were inducted. Further, in our region there has come into existence a pattern about clandestine acquisition of nuclear materials, missiles and related technologies. India, in this period, became the victim of externally aided and abetted terrorism, militancy and clandestine war through hired mercenaries.

The end of the Cold War marks a watershed in the history of the 20th century. While it has transformed the political landscape of Europe, it has done little to address India's security concerns. The relative order that was arrived at in Europe was not replicated in other parts of the globe.

At the global level, there is no evidence yet on the part of the nuclear weapon states to take decisive and irreversible steps in moving towards a nuclear-weapon-free world. Instead, the NPT has been extended indefinitely and unconditionally, perpetuating the existence of nuclear weapons in the hands of the five countries who are also permanent members of the UN Security Council. Some of these countries have doctrines that permit the first use of nuclear weapons; these countries are also engaged in programmes for modernisation of their nuclear arsenals.

Under such circumstances, India was left with little choice. It had to take necessary steps to ensure that the country's nuclear option, developed and safeguarded over decades, not be permitted to erode by a voluntary self-imposed restraint. Indeed, such an erosion would have had an irremediably adverse impact on our security. The Government was thus faced with a difficult decision. The only touchstone that guided it was national security. Tests conducted on 11 and 13 May are a continuation of the policies set into motion that put this country on the path of self-reliance and independence of thought and action. Nevertheless, there are certain moments when the chosen path reaches a fork and a decision has to be made. 1968 was one such moment in our nuclear chapter as were 1974 and 1996. At each of these moments, we took the right decision guided by national interest and supported by national consensus. 1998 was borne in the crucible of earlier decisions and made possible only because those decisions had been taken correctly in the past and in time.

At a time when developments in the area of advanced technologies are taking place at a breathtaking pace, new parameters need to be identified, tested and validated in order to ensure that skills remain contemporary and succeeding generations of scientists and engineers are able to build on the work done by their predecessors. The limited series of five tests undertaken by India was precisely such an exercise. It has achieved its stated objective. The data provided by these tests is critical to validate our capabilities in the design of nuclear weapons of different yields for different applications and different delivery systems. Further, these tests have significantly enhanced the capabilities of our scientists and engineers in computer simulation of new designs and enabled them to undertake sub-critical experiments in future, if considered necessary. In terms of technical capability, our scientists and engineers have the requisite resources to ensure a credible deterrent.

Our policies towards our neighbours and other countries too have not changed; India remains fully committed to the promotion of peace with stability, and resolution of all outstanding issues through bilateral dialogue and negotiations. These tests were not directed against any country; these were intended to reassure the people of India about their security and convey determination that this Government, like previous Governments, has the capability and resolve to safeguard their national security interests. The Government will continue to remain engaged in substantive dialogue with our neighbours to improve relations and to expand the scope of our interactions in a mutually advantageous manner. Confidence-building is a continuous process; we remain committed to it. Consequent upon the tests and arising from an insufficient appreciation of our security concerns, some countries have been persuaded to take steps that sadden us. We value our bilateral relations. We remain committed to dialogue and reaffirm that preservation of India's security create no conflict of interest with these countries.

India is a nuclear weapon state. This is a reality that cannot be denied. It is not a conferment that we seek; nor is it a status for others to grant. It is an endowment to the nation by our scientists and engineers. It is India's due, the right of one-sixth of humankind. Our strengthened capability adds to our sense of responsibility: the responsibility and obligation of power. India, mindful of its international obligations, shall not use these weapons to commit aggression or to mount threats against any country; these are weapons of self-defence and to ensure that in turn, India is also not subjected to nuclear threats or coercion. In 1994, we had proposed that India and Pakistan jointly undertake not to be the first to use their nuclear capability against each other. The Government on this occasion reiterates its readiness to discuss a "no-first-use" agreement with that country, as also with other countries bilaterally, or in a collective forum. India shall not engage in an arms race. India shall also not subscribe or reinvent the doctrines of the Cold War. India remains committed to the basic tenet of our foreign policy—a conviction that global elimination of nuclear weapons will enhance its security as well as that of the rest of the world. It will continue to urge countries, particularly other nuclear weapon states, to adopt measures that would contribute meaningfully to such an objective.

A number of initiatives have been taken in the past. In 1978, India proposed negotiations for an international convention that would prohibit the use or threat of use of nuclear weapons. This was followed by another initiative in 1982 calling for a 'nuclear freeze'—a prohibition on production of fissile materials for weapons, on production of nuclear weapons and related delivery systems. In 1988, we put forward an Action Plan for phased elimination of all nuclear weapons within a specified time frame. It is our regret that these proposals did not receive a positive response from other nuclear weapon states. Had their response been positive, India need not have gone for the current tests. This is where our approach to nuclear weapons is different from others. This difference is the cornerstone of our nuclear doctrine. It is marked by restraint and striving for the total elimination of all weapons of mass destruction.

We will continue to support such initiatives, taken individually or collectively by the Non-Aligned Movement which has continued to attach the highest priority to nuclear disarmament. This was reaffirmed most recently, last week, at the NAM Ministerial meeting held at Cartageña which has "reiterated their call on the Conference on Disarmament to establish, as the highest priority, an ad hoc committee to start in 1998 negotiations on a phased programme for the complete elimination of nuclear weapons with a specified framework of time, including a Nuclear Weapons Convention." The collective voice of 113 NAM countries reflects an approach to global nuclear disarmament to which India has remained committed. One of the NAM member initiatives to which we attach great importance was the reference to the International Court of Justice resulting in the unanimous declaration from the ICJ, as part of the Advisory Opinion handed down on 8 July 1996, that "there exists an obligation to pursue in good faith and bring to a conclusion negotiations leading to nuclear disarmament in all its aspects under strict and effective international control." India was one of the countries that appealed to the ICJ on this issue. No other nuclear weapon state has supported this judgement; in fact, they have sought to decry its value. We have been and will continue to be in the forefront of the calls for opening negotiations for a Nuclear Weapons Convention, so that this challenge can be dealt with in the same manner that we have dealt with the scourge of two other weapons of mass destruction—through the Biological Weapons Convention and the Chemical Weapons Convention. In keeping with our commitment to comprehensive, universal and non-discriminatory approaches to disarmament, India is an original State Party to both these Conventions. Accordingly, India will shortly submit the plan of destruction of its chemical weapons to the international authority—Organisation for the Prohibition of Chemical Weapons. We fulfil our obligations whenever we undertake them.

Traditionally, India has been an outward-looking country. Our strong commitment to multilateralism is reflected in our active participation in organisations like the United Nations. In recent years, in keeping with the new challenges, we have actively promoted regional cooperation—in SAARC, in the Indian Ocean Rim-Association for Regional Cooperation and as a member of the ASEAN Regional Forum. This engagement will also continue. The policies of economic liberalisation introduced in recent years have increased our regional and global linkages and the Government shall deepen and strengthen these ties.

Our nuclear policy has been marked by restraint and openness. It has not violated any international agreements either in 1974 or now, in 1998. Our concerns have been made known to our interlocutors in recent years. The restraint exercised for 24 years, after having demonstrated our capability in 1974, is in itself a unique example. Restraint, however, has to arise from strength. It cannot be based upon indecision or doubt. Restraint is valid only when doubts are removed. The series of tests undertaken by India have led to the removal of doubts. The action involved was balanced in that it was the minimum necessary to maintain what is an irreducible component of our national security calculus. This Government's decision has, therefore, to be seen as part of a tradition of restraint that has characterised our policy in the past 50 years.

Subsequent to the tests the Government has already stated that India will now observe a voluntary moratorium and refrain from conducting underground nuclear test explosions. It has also indicated willingness to move towards a de-jure formalisation of this declaration. The basic obligation of the CTBT are thus met: to refrain from undertaking nuclear test explosions. This voluntary declaration is intended to convey to the international community the seriousness of our intent for meaningful engagement. Subsequent decisions will be taken after assuring ourselves of the security needs of the country.

India has also indicated readiness to participate in negotiations in the Conference on Disarmament in Geneva on a Fissile Material Cut-off Treaty. The basic objective of this treaty is to prohibit future production of fissile materials for use in nuclear weapons or nuclear explosive devices. India's approach in these negotiations will be to ensure that this treaty emerges as a universal and non-discriminatory treaty, backed by an effective verification mechanism. When we embark on these negotiations, it shall be in the full confidence of the adequacy and credibility of the nation's weaponised nuclear deterrent.

India has maintained effective export controls on nuclear materials as well as related technologies even though we are neither a party to the NPT nor a member of the Nuclear Suppliers' Group. Nonetheless, India is committed to non-proliferation and the maintaining of stringent export controls to ensure that there is no leakage of our indigenously developed know-how and technologies. In fact, India's conduct in this regard has been better than some countries party to the NPT.

India has in the past conveyed our concerns on the inadequacies of the international nuclear non-proliferation regime. It has explained that the country was not in a position to join because the regime did not address our country's security concerns. These could have been addressed by moving towards global nuclear disarmament, our preferred approach. As this did not take place, India was obliged to stand aside from the emerging regime so that its freedom of action was not constrained. This is the precise path that has continued to be followed unwaveringly for the last three decades. That same constructive approach will underlie India's dialogue with countries that need to be persuaded of our serious intent and willingness to engage so that mutual concerns are satisfactorily addressed. The challenge to Indian statecraft is balancing and reconciling India's security imperatives with valid international concerns in this regard.

The House is aware of the different reactions that have emanated from the people of India and from different parts of the world. The overwhelming support of the citizens of India is a source of strength for the Government. It not only tells that this decision was right but also that the country wants a focussed leadership, which attends to national security needs. This the Government pledges to do as a sacred duty. The Government has also been greatly heartened by the outpouring of support from Indians abroad. They have, with one voice, spoken in favour of the Government's action. The Government conveys its profound gratitude to the citizens of India and to Indians abroad, and looks to them for support in the difficult period ahead.

In this, the fiftieth year of our independence, India stands at a defining moment in our history. The rationale for the Government's decision is based on the same policy tenets that have guided the country for five decades. These policies were sustained successfully because of the underlying national consensus. The present decision and future actions will continue to reflect a commitment to sensibilities and obligations of an ancient civilisation, a sense of responsibility and restraint, but a restraint born of the assurance of action, not of doubts or apprehension. The Gita explains (Chap. VI-3) as none other can. (This passage interprets as: Action is a process to reach a goal; action may reflect tumult but when measured and focussed, will yield its objective of stability and peace.)

STATEMENT MADE BY THE PRIME MINISTER OF PAKISTAN, MUHAMMAD NAWAZ SHARIF

May 28, 1998

Pakistan today successfully conducted five nuclear tests.

The results were as expected. There was no release of radio-activity. I congratulate all Pakistani scientists, engineers and technicians for their dedicated teamwork and expertise in mastering complex and advanced technologies. The entire nation takes justifiable pride in the accomplishments of the Pakistan Atomic Energy Commission, Dr. A.Q. Khan Research Laboratories and all affiliated Organizations. They have demonstrated Pakistan's ability to deter aggression.

Pakistan has been obliged to exercise the nuclear option due to weaponization of India's nuclear program. This had led to the collapse of the "existential deterrence" and had radically altered the strategic balance in our region. Immediately after its nuclear tests, India had brazenly raised the demand that "Islamabad should realize the change in the geo-strategic situation in the region" and threatened that "India will deal firmly and strongly with Pakistan."

Our security, and peace and stability of the entire region, was thus gravely threatened. As a self-respecting nation we had no choice left to us. Our hand was forced by the present Indian leadership's reckless actions. After due deliberation and a careful review of all options we took the decision to restore the strategic balance. The nation would not have expected anything less from its leadership. For the past three decades Pakistan repeatedly drew attention of the international community to India's incremental steps on the nuclear and ballistic ladder.

Our warnings remained unheeded. Despite the continuing deterioration in Pakistan's security environment, we exercised utmost restraint. We pursued in all earnest the goal of non-proliferation in South Asia. Our initiatives to keep South Asia free of nuclear and ballistic weapon systems were spurned. The international response to the Indian nuclear tests did not factor the security situation in our region. While asking us to exercise restraint, powerful voices urged acceptance of the Indian weaponization as a fait accompli.

Pakistan's legitimate security concerns were not addressed, even after the threat of use of nuclear weapons and nuclear blackmail. We could not have remained complacent about threats to our security. We could not have ignored the magnitude of the threat. Under no circumstances would the Pakistani nation compromise on matters pertaining to its life and existence. Our decision to exercise the nuclear option has been taken in the interest of national self-defense. These weapons are to deter aggression, whether nuclear or conventional.

Pakistan will continue to support the goals of nuclear disarmament and non-proliferation, especially in the Conference on Disarmament, bearing in mind the new realities. We are undertaking a re-evaluation of the applicability and relevance of the global non-proliferation regimes to nuclearized South Asia. We are ready to engage in a constructive dialogue with other countries, especially major powers, on ways and means to promoting these goals, in the new circumstances.

Pakistan has always acted with utmost restraint and responsibility. We will continue to do so in the future.

We are prepared to resume Pakistan-India dialogue to address all outstanding issues including the core issue for Jammu and Kashmir, as well as peace and security. These should include urgent steps for mutual restraint and equitable measures for nuclear stabilization.

Pakistan has already offered a non-aggression pact to India on the basis of a just settlement of the Jammu and Kashmir dispute. I would like to reiterate this offer.

We have instituted effective command and control structures. We are fully conscious of the need to handle these weapon systems with the highest sense of responsibility.

We have not and will not transfer sensitive technologies to other states or entities.

At the same time, Pakistan will oppose all unjust embargoes aimed at preventing it from exercising its right to develop various technologies for self-defense or peaceful purposes.

I would like to again assure all countries that our nuclear weapon systems are meant only for self-defense and there should be no apprehension or concern in this regard.

The Pakistani people are united in their resolve to safeguard, at all costs, Pakistan's independence, sovereignty and territorial integrity. I would like to congratulate the nation on the achievements of our scientists and engineers. They have made it possible for the people of Pakistan to enter the next century, with confidence in themselves and faith in their destiny.

P-5 JOINT COMMUNIQUÉ

China, France, Russia, United Kingdom, and the United States

June 4, 1998

1. Bearing in mind the responsibility of their countries for the maintenance of international peace and security, the Foreign Ministers of China, France, Russia, the United Kingdom and the United States met in Geneva on June 4, 1998, to coordinate their response to the grave situation created by the nuclear tests carried out in May 1998 by India and then by Pakistan. The Ministers condemned these tests, expressed their deep concern about the danger to peace and stability in the region, and pledged to cooperate closely in urgent efforts to prevent a nuclear and missile arms race in the Subcontinent, to bolster the non-proliferation regime, and to encourage reconciliation and peaceful resolution of differences between India and Pakistan.

2. The Ministers agreed that quick action is needed to arrest the further escalation of regional tensions stimulated by the recent nuclear tests. India and Pakistan should therefore stop all further such tests. They should refrain from the weaponization or deployment of nuclear weapons, from the testing or deployment of missiles capable of delivering nuclear weapons, and from any further production of fissile material for nuclear weapons. They should also halt provocative statements, refrain from any military movements that could be construed as threatening, and increase transparency in their actions. Direct communications between the parties could help to build confidence.

3. To reinforce security and stability in the region and more widely, the Five strongly believe that India and Pakistan should adhere to the Comprehensive Nuclear Test Ban Treaty immediately and unconditionally, thereby facilitating its early entry

into force. The Five also call upon India and Pakistan to participate, in a positive spirit and on the basis of the agreed mandate, in negotiations with other states in the Conference on Disarmament for a Fissile Material Cut-off Convention with a view to reaching early agreement. The Five will seek firm commitments by India and Pakistan not to weaponize or deploy nuclear weapons or missiles. India and Pakistan should also confirm their policies not to export equipment, materials or technology that could contribute to weapons of mass destruction or missiles capable of delivering them, and should undertake appropriate commitments in that regard.

4. The Ministers agreed that the international non-proliferation regime must remain strong and effective despite the recent nuclear tests in South Asia. Their goal continues to be adherence by all countries, including India and Pakistan, to the Nuclear Non-Proliferation Treaty (NPT) as it stands, without any modification. This Treaty is the cornerstone of the non-proliferation regime and the essential foundation for the pursuit of nuclear disarmament. Notwithstanding their recent nuclear tests, India and Pakistan do not have the status of nuclear weapons states in accordance with the NPT.

5. The Ministers concluded that efforts to resolve disputes between India and Pakistan must be pursued with determination. The Ministers affirm their readiness to assist India and Pakistan, in a manner acceptable to both sides, in promoting reconciliation and cooperation. The Ministers pledged that they will actively encourage India and Pakistan to find mutually acceptable solutions, through direct dialogue, that address the root causes of the tension, including Kashmir, and to try to build confidence rather than seek confrontation. In that connection, the Ministers urged both parties to avoid threatening military movements, cross-border violations, or other provocative acts.

6. The Ministers also considered what actions the Five could take, individually or collectively, to foster peace and security in

South Asia. They will encourage India and Pakistan to adopt practical measures to prevent an arms race. They confirmed their respective policies to prevent the export of equipment, materials or technology that could in any way assist programmes in India or Pakistan for nuclear weapons or for ballistic missiles capable of delivering such weapons. They also undertook to do all they could to facilitate a reduction of tensions between those states, and to provide assistance, at the request of both parties, in the development and implementation of confidence- and security-building measures. They remain determined to fulfill their commitments relating to nuclear disarmament under Article VI of the NPT.

7. The Ministers viewed their meeting in Geneva as setting in motion a process aimed at strengthening peace and stability in South Asia, at encouraging restraint by India and Pakistan, at promoting the resolution of outstanding differences, and at bolstering the international non-proliferation regime. They will remain fully engaged in pursuing these goals, and will work actively to build broad support in the international community for the objectives they agreed today.

U.N. SECURITY COUNCIL RESOLUTION 1172

Adopted by the Security Council

June 6, 1998

The Security Council,

Reaffirming the statements of its President of 14 May 1998 (S/PRST/1998/12) and of 29 May 1998 (S/PRST/1998/17),

Reiterating the statement of its President of 31 January 1992 (S/23500), which stated, *inter alia,* that the proliferation of all weapons of mass destruction constitutes a threat to international peace and security,

Gravely concerned at the challenge that the nuclear tests conducted by India and then by Pakistan constitute to international efforts aimed at strengthening the global regime of non-proliferation of nuclear weapons, and *also gravely concerned* at the danger to peace and stability in the region,

Deeply concerned at the risk of a nuclear arms race in South Asia, and *determined* to prevent such a race,

Reaffirming the crucial importance of the Treaty on the Non-Proliferation of Nuclear Weapons and the Comprehensive Nuclear Test Ban Treaty for global efforts towards nuclear non-proliferation and nuclear disarmament,

Recalling the Principles and Objectives for Nuclear Non-Proliferation and Disarmament adopted by the 1995 Review and Extension Conference of the Parties to the Treaty on the Non-Proliferation of Nuclear Weapons, and the successful outcome of that Conference,

Affirming the need to continue to move with determination towards the full realization and effective implementation of all the provisions of the Treaty on the Non-Proliferation of Nuclear Weapons, and *welcoming* the determination of the five nuclear-weapon States to fulfil their commitments relating to nuclear disarmament under Article VI of that Treaty,

Mindful of its primary responsibility under the Charter of the United Nations for the maintenance of international peace and security,

1. *Condemns* the nuclear tests conducted by India on 11 and 13 May 1998 and by Pakistan on 28 and 30 May 1998;

2. *Endorses* the Joint Communiqué issued by the Foreign Ministers of China, France, the Russian Federation, the United Kingdom of Great Britain and Northern Ireland and the United States of America at their meeting in Geneva on 4 June 1998 (S/1998/473);

3. *Demands* that India and Pakistan refrain from further nuclear tests and in this context *calls upon* all States not to carry out any nuclear weapon test explosion or any other nuclear explosion in accordance with the provisions of the Comprehensive Nuclear Test Ban Treaty;

4. *Urges* India and Pakistan to exercise maximum restraint and to avoid threatening military movements, cross-border violations, or other provocations in order to prevent an aggravation of the situation;

5. *Urges* India and Pakistan to resume the dialogue between them on all outstanding issues, particularly on all matters pertaining to peace and security, in order to remove the tensions between them, and *encourages* them to find mutually acceptable solutions that address the root causes of those tensions, including Kashmir;

6. *Welcomes* the efforts of the Secretary-General to encourage India and Pakistan to enter into dialogue;

7. *Calls upon* India and Pakistan immediately to stop their nuclear weapon development programmes, to refrain from

weaponization or from the deployment of nuclear weapons, to cease development of ballistic missiles capable of delivering nuclear weapons and any further production of fissile material for nuclear weapons, to confirm their policies not to export equipment, materials or technology that could contribute to weapons of mass destruction or missiles capable of delivering them and to undertake appropriate commitments in that regard;

8. *Encourages* all States to prevent the export of equipment, materials or technology that could in any way assist programmes in India or Pakistan for nuclear weapons or for ballistic missiles capable of delivering such weapons, and *welcomes* national policies adopted and declared in this respect;

9. *Expresses* its grave concern at the negative effect of the nuclear tests conducted by India and Pakistan on peace and stability in South Asia and beyond;

10. *Reaffirms* its full commitment to and the crucial importance of the Treaty on the Non-Proliferation of Nuclear Weapons and the Comprehensive Nuclear Test Ban Treaty as the cornerstones of the international regime on the non-proliferation of nuclear weapons and as essential foundations for the pursuit of nuclear disarmament;

11. *Expresses* its firm conviction that the international regime on the non-proliferation of nuclear weapons should be maintained and consolidated and *recalls* that in accordance with the Treaty on the Non-Proliferation of Nuclear Weapons India or Pakistan cannot have the status of a nuclear-weapon State;

12. *Recognizes* that the tests conducted by India and Pakistan constitute a serious threat to global efforts towards nuclear non-proliferation and disarmament;

13. *Urges* India and Pakistan, and all other States that have not yet done so, to become Parties to the Treaty on the Non-Proliferation of Nuclear Weapons and to the Comprehensive Nuclear Test Ban Treaty without delay and without conditions;

14. *Urges* India and Pakistan to participate, in a positive spirit and on the basis of the agreed mandate, in negotiations at the Conference on Disarmament in Geneva on a treaty banning the production of fissile material for nuclear weapons or other nuclear explosive devices, with a view to reaching early agreement;

15. *Requests* the Secretary-General to report urgently to the Council on the steps taken by India and Pakistan to implement the present resolution;

16. *Expresses* its readiness to consider further how best to ensure the implementation of the present resolution;

17. *Decides* to remain actively seized of the matter.

G-8 FOREIGN MINISTERS COMMUNIQUÉ ON INDIAN AND PAKISTANI NUCLEAR TESTS

Canada, France, Germany, Italy, Japan, Russia, United Kingdom, and the United States

June 12, 1998

1. We, the Foreign Ministers of eight major industrialised democracies and the Representative of the European Commission, held a special meeting in London on 12 June 1998 to consider the serious global challenge posed by the nuclear tests carried out by India and Pakistan. Recalling the statement issued by our Heads of State or Government on 15 May, and emphasizing the support of all of us for the communiqué issued by the P5 in Geneva on 4 June and United Nations Security Council Resolution 1172, we condemn the nuclear tests carried out by India on 11 and 13 May 1998 and by Pakistan on 28 May and 30 May. These tests have affected both countries' relationships with each of us, worsened rather than improved their security environment, damaged their prospects of achieving their goals of sustainable economic development, and run contrary to global efforts towards nuclear non-proliferation and nuclear disarmament.

2. The negative impact of these tests on the international standing and ambitions of both countries will be serious and lasting. They will also have a serious negative impact on investor confidence. Both countries need to take positive actions directed towards defusing tension in the region and rejoining the international community's efforts towards non-proliferation and nuclear disarmament. Urgent action is needed both to halt an arms race on the Sub-Continent, which would divert resources from urgent economic priorities, and to reduce tension, build confidence and encourage peaceful res-

olution of the differences between India and Pakistan, so that their peoples may face a better future.

3. With a view to halting the nuclear and missile arms race on the Sub-Continent, and taking note of the official statements of the Indian and Pakistani Governments that they wish to avoid such an arms race, we consider that India and Pakistan should immediately take the following steps, already endorsed by the United Nations Security Council:

— stop all further nuclear tests and adhere to the Comprehensive Nuclear Test Ban Treaty immediately and unconditionally, thereby facilitating its early entry into force;

— refrain from weaponisation or deployment of nuclear weapons and from the testing or deployment of missiles capable of delivering nuclear weapons, and enter into firm commitments not to weaponize or deploy nuclear weapons or missiles;

— refrain from any further production of fissile material for nuclear weapons or other nuclear explosive devices and participate, in a positive spirit and on the basis of the agreed mandate, in negotiations with other states in the Conference on Disarmament for a Fissile Material Cut-Off Convention with a view to reaching early agreement;

— confirm their policies not to export equipment, materials and technology that could contribute to weapons of mass destruction or missiles capable of delivering them, and undertake appropriate commitments in that regard.

We believe that such action would be strongly in the interest of both countries.

4. With a view to reducing tension, building confidence and encouraging peaceful resolution of their differences through dialogue, India and Pakistan should:

— undertake to avoid threatening military movements, cross-border violations, including infiltrations or hot pursuit, or other provocative acts and statements;

— discourage terrorist activity and any support for it;

— implement fully the confidence- and security-building measures they have already agreed and develop further such measures;

— resume without delay a direct dialogue that addresses the root causes of the tension, including Kashmir, through such measures as early resumption of Foreign Secretary level talks, effective use of the hot-line between the two leaders, and realisation of a meeting between Prime Ministers on the occasion of the 10th SAARC Summit scheduled next month;

— allow and encourage progress towards enhanced Indo-Pakistani economic cooperation, including a free trade area in South Asia.

We encourage the development of a regional security dialogue.

5. We pledge actively to encourage India and Pakistan to find mutually acceptable solutions to their problems and stand ready to assist India and Pakistan in pursuing any of these positive actions. Such assistance might be provided, at the request of both parties, in the development and implementation of confidence- and security-building measures.

6. The recent nuclear tests by India and Pakistan do not change the definition of a nuclear weapon state in the NPT, and therefore, notwithstanding those tests, India and Pakistan do not have the status of nuclear weapon states in accordance with the NPT. We continue to urge India and Pakistan to adhere to the NPT as it stands, without any conditions. We shall continue to apply firmly our respective policies to prevent the export of materials, equipment or technology that could in any way

assist programmes in India or Pakistan for nuclear weapons or for ballistic missiles capable of delivering such weapons.

7. It is our firm view that the nuclear tests by India and Pakistan reinforce the importance of maintaining and strengthening the Nuclear Non-Proliferation Treaty as the cornerstone of the non-proliferation regime and as the essential foundation for the pursuit of nuclear disarmament. We all, nuclear weapon states and non-nuclear weapon states alike, reiterate our determination to fulfil the commitments relating to nuclear disarmament under Article VI of the NPT. These commitments were reaffirmed at the 1995 NPT Review and Extension Conference and included the determined pursuit by the nuclear weapon states of systematic and progressive efforts to reduce nuclear weapons globally with the ultimate goal of eliminating those weapons. We note the progress already made in this direction and welcome the firm intention both of the United States and the Russian Federation to bring START II into force, and to negotiate and conclude a START III agreement at the earliest possible date. We also note contributions made by other nuclear weapon states to the reductions process. We call upon all states to sign and ratify the Comprehensive Nuclear Test Ban Treaty rapidly to ensure its entry into force, and welcome the determination of the member governments of the G8 that have not yet ratified the Treaty to do so at the earliest possible date. We continue to look for the accession to the NPT of the remaining countries which are not yet parties to it.

8. We call on all the member states of the Conference on Disarmament to agree on the immediate opening of the Cut-Off negotiation at the CD.

9. Both India and Pakistan face enormous challenges in developing their economies and building prosperity. However, the recent nuclear tests have created an atmosphere of regional instability which will undermine the region's attractiveness to both foreign and domestic investment, damaging business confidence and the prospects for economic growth. The diversion

of their resources to nuclear and other weapons programmes displaces more productive investment and weakens their ability to pursue sound economic policies. It calls into question the commitment of both governments to poverty reduction and undermines the regional cooperation between SAARC countries on social and economic issues. In line with the approach to development set out in the Naples, Lyon, Denver and Birmingham Communiqués, we call on both governments to reduce expenditure that undermines their objective of promoting sound economic policies that will benefit all members of society, especially the poorest, and to otherwise enhance cooperation in South Asia.

10. We believe it is important that India and Pakistan are aware of the strength of the international community's views on their recent tests and on these other subjects. Several among us have, on a unilateral basis, taken specific actions to underscore our strong concerns. All countries should act as they see fit to demonstrate their displeasure and address their concerns to India and Pakistan as a result of actions by their governments, and we will therefore not oppose loans by international financial institutions to the two countries to meet basic human needs. We agree, however, to work for a postponement in consideration of other loans in the World Bank and other international financial institutions to India and Pakistan, and to any other country that will conduct nuclear tests.

11. We pledge to convey the common views of our Governments on these matters to those of India and Pakistan with a view to bringing about early and specific progress in the areas outlined above. We plan to keep developments under review and to continue the process of pursuing the goals on which we are all agreed.

FACT SHEET: INDIA AND PAKISTAN SANCTIONS RELEASED BY THE U.S. DEPARTMENT OF STATE, BUREAU OF ECONOMIC AND AGRICULTURAL AFAIRS

June 18, 1998

The United States imposed sanctions on India and Pakistan as a result of their nuclear tests in May. In imposing these sanctions, we seek:
- to send a strong message to would-be nuclear testers;
- to have maximum influence on Indian and Pakistani behavior;
- to target the governments, rather than the people; and,
- to minimize the damage to other U.S. interests.

Our goals are that India and Pakistan:
- halt further nuclear testing;
- sign the Comprehensive Test Ban Treaty (CTBT) immediately and without conditions;
- not deploy or test missiles or nuclear weapons;
- cut off fissile material production for nuclear weapons;
- cooperate in Fissile Material Cut-off Treaty (FMCT) negotiations in Geneva;
- maintain and formalize restraints on sharing sensitive goods and technologies with other countries; and,
- reduce bilateral tensions, including Kashmir.

Accordingly, the United States:
- Terminated or suspended foreign assistance under the Foreign Assistance Act, with exceptions provided by law (e.g., humanitarian assistance, food, or other agricultural commodities).
  — $21 million in economic development assistance and housing guarantee authority for India terminated.

[66]

— $6 million Greenhouse Gas program in India suspended.
— Trade Development Agency will not consider new projects.
— Most assistance to Pakistan had already been prohibited.

- Terminated foreign military sales under the Arms Export Control Act, and revoked licenses for the commercial sale of any item on the U.S. munitions list.
  — Suspended delivery of previously approved defense articles and services to India.

- Halted any new commitments of USG credits and credit guarantees by USG entities (EXIM, OPIC, CCC).
  — The Administration will support legislation to permit CCC credits for food and agricultural commodities.
  — OPIC had only recently reopened in Pakistan; however, India was one of OPIC's top five countries receiving an average of $300 million annually in OPIC support.
  — EXIM had only recently reopened in Pakistan with one expression of interest pending for $1.1 million; $500 million in pending financing in India will not go forward.

- Gained G-8 support to postpone consideration of non-basic human needs (BHN) loans for India and Pakistan by the International Financial Institutions (IFI) to bolster the effect of the Glenn amendment requirement that the U.S. oppose non-BHN IFI loans.
  — $1.17 billion in IFI lending postponed for India.
  — although no IFI loans for Pakistan have been presented for board consideration, $25 million in IMF assistance has been postponed for failure to meet economic benchmarks.

- Will issue Executive Orders to prohibit U.S. banks from extending loans or credits to the Governments of India and Pakistan.

- Will deny export of all dual-use items controlled for nuclear or missile reasons. Will presume denial for all other dual-use exports to entities involved in nuclear or missile programs.

— will toughen existing controls for government military entities;
— will continue denial of nuclear exports licensed by NRC or
  authorized by DOE; and
— will continue to favorably consider on a case-by-case basis
  other transactions which do not support nuclear, missile, or
  inappropriate military activities.

Other Reports of Independent Task Forces
Sponsored by the Council on Foreign Relations

* †*Managing Change on the Korean Peninsula* (1998)
Morton I. Abramowitz and James T. Laney, Co-Chairs; Michael J. Green, Project Director

*†*Promoting U.S. Economic Relations with Africa* (1998)
Peggy Dulany and Frank Savage, Co-Chairs; Salih Booker, Project Manager

* †*Differentiated Containment: U.S. Policy Toward Iran and Iraq* (1997)
Zbigniew Brzezinski and Brent Scowcroft, Co-Chairs

†*Russia, Its Neighbors, and an Enlarging NATO* (1997)
Richard G. Lugar, Chair

* †*Financing America's Leadership: Protecting American Interests and Promoting American Values* (1997)
Mickey Edwards and Stephen J. Solarz, Co-Chairs

**Rethinking International Drug Control: New Directions for U.S. Policy* (1997)
Mathea Falco, Chair

†*A New U.S. Policy Toward India and Pakistan* (1997)
Richard N. Haass, Chairman; Gideon Rose, Project Director

Arms Control and the U.S.-Russian Relationship: Problems, Prospects, and Prescriptions (1996)
Robert D. Blackwill, Chairman and Author; Keith W. Dayton, Project Director

†*American National Interests and the United Nations* (1996)
George Soros, Chairman

†*Making Intelligence Smarter: The Future of U.S. Intelligence* (1996)
Maurice R. Greenberg, Chairman; Richard N. Haass, Project Director

†*Lessons of the Mexican Peso Crisis* (1996)
John C. Whitehead, Chairman; Marie-Josée Kravis, Project Director

†*Non-Lethal Technologies: Military Options and Implications* (1995)
Malcolm H. Wiener, Chairman

Managing the Taiwan Issue: Key Is Better U.S. Relations with China (1995)
Stephen Friedman, Chairman; Elizabeth Economy, Project Director

†*Should NATO Expand?* (1995)
Harold Brown, Chairman; Charles Kupchan, Project Director

---

*Available from Brookings Institution Press ($5.00 per copy). To order, call 1-800-275-1447.
†Available on the Council on Foreign Relations homepage at www. foreign relations. org.